मृगजल पे बहती कश्ती

mrigjal pe behtee kashtee

Sailing On A Mirage

मृगजल पे बहती कश्ती

— mrigjal pe behtee kashtee —

Sailing On A Mirage

VIJAY FAFAT

WALKING STICK PUBLICATION

WALKING STICK PUBLICATION

ISBN-13: 978-981-11-7523-7

Published by Walking Stick Publication, Singapore

Author Contact
Email : vijayfafat@gmail.com
Website : www.vijayfafat.wordpress.com
Amazon : www.amazon.com/author/vijayfafat

About The Book
Book Concept : Vijay Fafat
Image Selection : Vijay Fafat
Book Layout : Abhishek Tiwari
Design Website : www.CreativeKindles.com

First Printing: June, 2018

“ साकी इस बोतल से आज वो मृगजल बहा दे
एक भूली-बिसरी बातों की नैय्या लाया हूँ साथ ”

Contents

Devnagari Pronunciation Key

The Appendix has a short primer on the Devnagari script. Below is the key to reading this book in transliterated form in case the reader is unfamiliar with it. While there are many technical transliteration schemes available, we have chosen to devise the one below to follow intuitive phonetic representation based on the English alphabet, which suffices for our purpose.

Symbol	**Devnagari**	**Pronunciation**
a	अ	Starting sound in "against"
aa	आ	Starting sound in "after"
ai	ऐ	Starting sound of "air"
au	ऑ	Starting sound in "awful"
b	ब	Starting sound of "burn"
bau	बौ	Combination of 2 sounds: "b" and "au"
bh	भ	Combination of 2 sounds: "b" and "h"
br	ब्र	Combination of 2 sounds: "b" and "r"
ch	च	Starting sound in "chatter"
chai	चै	Combination of 2 sounds: "ch" and "ai"
chau	चौ	Combination of 2 sounds: "ch" and "au"
Chh, Chha	छ	Combination of 2 sounds: "ch" and "h"
Chhaa	छा	Combination of 2 sounds: "Chh" and "aa"
d	द	Same as the British pronunciation of English word, "the"
D	ड	Starting sound in "dog"
dh	ध	Combination of 2 sounds: "d" and "h"
Dh	ढ	Combination of 2 sounds: "D" and "h"
dhau	धौ	Combination of 2 sounds: "dh" and "au"
dhe	धे	Combination of 2 sounds: "dh" and "e"
Dhe	ढे	Combination of 2 sounds: "Dh" and "e"
e	ए	Last sound in "lay". If in doubt, think of "e" replaced by "A", the first sound while reciting A B C D…
-e-	ए	Last sound in "lay", appears in conjoining 2 words - e.g. "ummeed-e-nazar"
ee	ई	Starting sound in "keep"
f, fa	फ	Starting sound of "first"

g	ग	Starting sound in "gutter"
ge	गे	Same as the pronunciation of "gay"
gh	घ	Combination of 2 sounds: "g" and "h"
h, ha	ह	Starting sound in "hunger". Remember that "ha" is NOT "haa" as in "haha". It is the starting sound in "hunger"
hai	है	Combination of 2 sounds: "h" and "ai". This is a very common word in Hindi and means some form of "is", "exists", "is around", and the like
hee	ही	Combination of 2 sounds: "h" and "ee"
i	इ	Clipped "ee" sound, as in "lit"
j	ज	Starting sound of "jug"
jh, jha	झ	Combination of 2 sounds: "j" and "h"
jhee	झी	Combination of 2 sounds: "j" and "hee"
jho	झो	Combination of 2 sounds: "j" and "ho"
k	क	Starting sound of "cut"
kai	कै	Combination of 2 sounds: "k" and "ai"
kh, kha	ख	Combination of 2 sounds: "k" and "h". The starting sound in "Khalifa", as in "Burj Khalifa"
khai	खै	Combination of 3 sounds - "k", "h" and "ai"
knee	नी	Combination of 3 sounds: "k" and "n" & "ee"
ksh	क्ष	Combination of 2 sounds: "k" and "sh"
kyo	क्यो	Starting sound in "Kyoto". Combination of 2 sounds: "k" and yo"
kyo.n	क्यों	Combination of 2 sounds: "kyo" and ".n". It means "why?" in Hindi
l, la	ल	Starting sound of "loud"
m	म	Starting sound of "mother"
ma	मा	Starting sound of "march"
mai	मै	Combination of 2 sounds: "m" and "ai". This does not mean "I". It is used in combination with other letters
mai.n	मैं	Combination of 3 sounds: "m", "ai" and ".n". mai.n means "I"
mm	म्म	Combination of 2 "m" sounds, with the first "m" clipped. Imagine pronouncing "humming" but as 2

		separate words, "hum" and "ming". The "m sound which emerges is the "mm" sound
n	न	Starting sound in "no"
.n	-	nasal "n", merging with the prior syllable, as in the “n” sound in “anger”. It appears as a dot or an upward opening semi circle with its center dot. It only appears above some Hindi letter, never stand-alone. e.g. "maa.n" is written as माँ and means "mother". It is a combination of the "maa" sound, at the end of which, the nasal "n" slides in, merging with the "aa" sound
N	ण	This has no English equivalent or combination. It is a strong "n". See comment. Make the "n" sound with the tip of the tongue touching the palate (the roof of the mouth). That is "N"
nn	न	Combination of 2 "n" sounds, with the first "n" clipped
nya, ny	न्य	Combination of 2 sounds: "n" and "ya"
oo	ऊ	Starting sound in "ooze"
p	प	Starting sound of "punch"
pai	पै	Combination of 2 sounds: "p" and "ai"
pe	पे	Combination of 2 sounds: "p" and "-e-"
pya, py	प्य	Combination of 2 sounds: "p" and "ya"
r	र	Starting sound of "run"
rau	रौ	Combination of 2 sounds: "r" and "au"
s	स	Starting sound in "sound"
se	से	Combination of 2 sounds: "s" and "-e-"
sh	श	Starting sound of "shut"
T	ट	Starting sound in "try"
t	त	Starting sound in "Talmud" or the French "tu"
Th	ठ	Combination of 2 sounds: "T" and "h"
th	थ	Starting sound in "three" or "thunder"
u	उ	A clipped "oo" sound
v	व	Starting sound of "viral"
w	व	Starting sound of "well"
ya, y	य	Starting sound in "yearn"
yo	यो	Starting sound of "yoke"
z	ज़	Last sound in "maze"

प्रस्तावना

ज्ञानी संत कह गये हैं की संसार एक मिथ्या है। एक दौड़ती परछाई जिसका कोई साझेदार नहीं। एक मृगजल जिसमे हम सारे प्राणी विलीन हैं, बिन ख़याल के की इस मृगजल से कभी किसीकी तृष्णा नहीं बुझी है। दुनिया एक भ्रम है जिसे हम सबने एक टाँके से बाँध रखा है। एक कोशिश करो तो शायद ये तिलिस्म टूट जाए...

उनकी बातों का सार तो यही समझ आया, की:

दो शब्दों का खेल ये, दो अर्थों की बाणी
जो समझा सो संत हुआ, बाकी मूढ़ीत प्राणी

ऐसा ज्ञानी कहते हैं।

अब सब तो ज्ञानी हो नहीं सकते। बाकीयों को रोज़–मर्रा की ज़िंदगी काटनी है। वही ज़िंदगी, जिसमे चाहे राजा गा रहा हो या रंक, उसके त्रितालवाले सुर सर्वधर्मसमःप्राय के समान गिने–चुने धुनों पर ही निकलते हैं। कुछ विडंबनाएँ, कुछ विषमता, कुछ शर्म, कुछ नाराज़गी। कुछ अंधविश्वास के साए। कुछ प्रेम–इश्क की गाथाएँ। ढलती शाम और अंगड़ाई लेती प्रहर के अफ़साने। रणभूमी, प्रणयभूमी और रंगभूमी पर शहादत। बस यही बातें हैं।

रहना इसी मृगजल में है। इसी रेगिस्तान मे कारवाँ चलाना है। कुछ गम के काफिले झेलने हैं, कुछ मुस्कुराहटों को आँगन में बिखेरना है। भाईचारा सभी का है, तो दुश्मनी भी दूर नहीं। यहीं पर मरना है – चाहे वो आँखों के पैने वार से हो, चाहे कर्कश वचनों के खंजर से। यही ज़िंदगी का अटूट सच है।

हर शक्स अपनी छोटी सी कश्ती को इस नश्वर दुनिया के मृगजल पर जी–जान से चला रहा है – इस इत्मिनान से की उस पार के साहिल पर मंज़िल है। अब कितनों ने नैय्या पार लगाई है वहाँ पहुँच कर इसका तो अल्लाह ही मालिक है...। चप्पू कई हैं इस्तेमाल में – *इश्क, रोष, जोश, याराना, झगड़े, रुसवाई, तन्हाई, यादें, भूक, ईर्ष्या, द्वेष, लालच, लालसा, ख़ौफ़,...।* हर ढलती शाम में इन पतवारों की महफ़िल लगती

है। किसी की गहमा–गहमी अंतर्मन के मायूस कोने मे ध्यान लगाती है तो किसी की झूमती मधुशाला में मसरूफ़ होती है। इस जमघट में साकी कुछ हमको पिलाता है, कुछ हम साकी को पीला देते हैं। गर मस्ती में झूमना दोनो की किस्मत में है, तो उदासी भी उसी खुली बोतल से बहती नज़र आती है।

उसी नैय्या, उसी बोतल की कुछ बहकी बातों की लिखा–पढ़ाई की है इन कोरे काग़ज़ों पर। एक छोटा सा पैगाम ... इस मृगजल क़ी कश्ती का... आपकी कश्ती के नाम...। बहते–बहते कुछ शौकीन शरीफों की महफ़िल में पहुँच कर कुछ रंगीनीयाँ बिखेर देंगी ये बातें, यही एक दिलासा है।

शब्बखैर!

विजय फाफट
सिंगापूर
मई 17, 2018

prastaavanaa

gyaanee sant keh gaye hai.n kee sansaar ek mithyaa hai | ek dauDtee parChhaa-ee jiskaa ko-ee saajhedaar nahi.n | ek mrigjal jisme ham saare praaNee vileen hai.n, bin khayaal ke kee is mrigjal se kabhee kiseekee trishNaa nahi.n bujhee hai | duniyaa ek bhram hai jise ham sabne ek Taa. nke se baandh rakhaa hai | ek koshish karo to shaayad ye tilism TooT jaa-e |

unkee baato.n kaa saar to yahee samajh aayaa, kee:

do shabdo.n kaa khel ye, do artho.n kee baaNee
jo samjhaa so sant hu-aa, baakee mooDhit praaNee

aisaa gyaanee kehte hai.n |

ab sab to gyaanee ho nahi.n sakte | baakiyo.n ko roz-marraa kee zindagee kaaTnee hai | wahee zindagee, jisme chaahe raajaa gaa rahaa ho yaa rank, unke tritaalwaale sur sarvadharma sama-h-praay ke samaan gine-chune dhuno.n par hee nikalte hai.n | kuChh viDambanaaye.n, kuChh vishamtaa, kuChh sharm, kuChh naaraazgee | kuChh andhavishwaas ke saaye | kuChh prem-ishk kee gaathaaye.n | Dhaltee shaam aur angDaayee letee prahar ke afsaane | raNbhoomee, praNaybhoomee aur rangbhoomee pe shahaadat | bas yahee bate.n hai.n |

rehnaa isee mrigjal me.n hai | isee registaan me kaarvaa.n chalaanaa hai | kuChh gam ke kaafile jhelne hai.n, kuChh muskuraahaTo.n ko aa.ngan me.n bikhernaa hai | bhaichaaraa sabhee kaa hai, to dushmanee bhee door nahi.n | yahi.n par marnaa hai - chaahe wo aa.nkho.n ke paine vaar se ho, chaahe karkash vachano.n ke khanjar se | yahee zindagee kaa aTooT sach hai |

har shaks apnee ChhoTee see kashtee ko is nashwar duniyaa ke mrigjal par jee-jaan se chalaa rahaa hai - is itminaan se kee us paar ke saahil par manzil hai | ab kitno.n ne naiyyaa paar lagaayee hai vahaa.n pahu.nch kar iskaa to allaah hee maalik hai... | chappoo ka-ee hai.n istemaal me.n - *ishk, rosh, josh, josh, yaaraanaa, jhagDe, ruswaaee, tanhaaee, yade.n, bhook, eershyaa, dvesh, laalach, laalsaa, khauf,...* | har Dhaltee shaam me.n in patwaaro.n kee mehfil lagtee hai | kisee kee gehmaa-gehmee antarman ke maayoos kone me.n dhyaan lagaatee hai to kisee kee jhoomtee madhushaalaa me.n masroof hotee hai | is jamghat me.n saakee kuChh hamko pilaataa hai, kuChh ham saakee ko pilaa dete hai.n | gar mastee me.n jhoomnaa dono ki kismat me.n hai, to udaasee bhee usee khulee botal se behtee nazar aatee hai |

usee naiyyaa, usee botal kee kuChh behkee baato.n kee likhaa-paDhaaee kee hai in kore kaagazo.n par | ek ChhoTaa saa paigaam... is mrigjal kee kashtee kaa... aapkee kashtee ke naam... | behte-behte kuChh shaukeen shareefo.n kee mehfil me.n pahu.nch kar kuChh ra.ngeeneeyaa.n bikher de.ngee ye baate.n, yahee ek dilaasaa hai |

shabba-khair!

Vijay Fafat
Singapore
May 17, 2018

Foreword (translated)

Men of wisdom have theorized that the world is a myth spun on the loom of imagination, a fleeting shadow which has never been a faithful companion to anyone for long. We are all immersed in a mirage, without the essential awareness that no water can be drawn from this mirage to quench our thirst. The world around us is a tapestry of illusion woven by our collective delusion, hanging by a thread; perhaps, if we tugged at the loose ends just a litttle harder, we might free ourselves of its pervading veil and understand the true nature of existence. The essence of all their teachings appears to highlight the *double entendre* which is life:

A game of few words, this life;
a fugue of dual thoughts;
he who deciphers... liberated the soul;
the rest they suffer the web this life has wrought...

This is, of course, what wise men say.

Now, not everyone has the luxury to indulge in such airy-fairy wisdom. The commoner has to deal with the quotidian vagaries of this world; that same worldly life which, in its egalitarian sweep, shows that a king and a pauper often sing the same, limited tunes which comprise the plebeian existence - a few moral dilemmas; a few discriminating inqualities; a modicum of shyness and shame; a supply of bile and anger; some tangled alleyways of blind faith; a few ballads of love and lust; the lore of twilight and dusk, the lazy renewal of a rising dawn; storied martyrdom on the battlefields of twined relationships, elaborate schemes of love and life's unfolding dramas - that is all there is to life.

Stay submerged we need to, per force, in this mirage. Drive our caravan we must, per force, in this vast desert. A few processions of grief, a few scattered drops of joy in our courtyard - that is all we have. If life offers an inclusive brotherhood, it also pours liberally the wine of poisoned relationships. Death by a thousand cuts is always in the offing - whether those cuts are delivered by teasing, arching eyes, or by the sharp knives of a lashing tongue. This, my friend, is the sole, unshakeable truth of life.

Every soul is rowing his little skiff with all his heart on this mirage of fleeting existence. Each is convinced that salvation lies on the other side of these false waters (though only the good Lord keeps the secret of such final enlightenment). Many are the oars we employ to sail forward - love, anger, enthusiasm, friendship, quarrels, petulance, melancholy, nostalgia, hunger, jealousy, spite, greed, desire. Every dusk brings with it a celebration of these oars. For some, the revelry meditates in the melancholy of inner thoughts; for others, it unfurls with abandon in drunken parties. In all such gatherings, sometimes the sommelier makes us quaff the wine of life, sometimes we turn the bottles on the sommelier. If intoxication is part of their lives, so is the sadness which flows out of the same bottle of grief.

Here, then, is that same paper boat, the same goblet of inebriated thoughts carved onto some blank pages. A minor missive from my ship of ephemeral fancy to yours... The one consolation arises from the hope that these ruminations will float into some drunken soiree somewhere, and their mellow wine may bring some cheer to the few revelers of life.

Wishing you good tidings at eventide!

Vijay Fafat
Singapore
May 17, 2018

मृगजल पे बहती कश्ती

—— mrigjal pe behtee kashtee ——

Sailing On A Mirage

VIJAY FAFAT

WALKING STICK PUBLICATION

Chhalkaa saagar

fer ke ummeed-e-nazar pe paanee,
wo pooChhe.n kyo.n chal diye mehfil se pyaase ...

Untippled

She douses the flames of desire in my eyes,
and asks why I leave the soirée so thirsty…

Chhalkaa = छलका = spilt

saagar = साग़र = "a goblet", in Urdu. In Hindi, the word means "sea".

mehfil = महफ़िल = gathering; a party, typically in the evening

छलका साग़र

फेर के उम्मीदे–नज़र पे पानी,
वो पूछें क्यों चल दिए महफ़िल से प्यासे...

charche

ye kyaa keh diyaa aapne chalte chalte
ab sau matlab nikle.nge aapke jaane ke baad…

Insinuation

The trail of careless words you left behind...
Oh! The havoc they are to wreak!
A hundred different rumors will they instigate now;
A myriad meanings will now take root in my mind…

matlab = मतलब = essence; understanding; meaning

चर्चे

ये क्या कह दिया आपने चलते चलते
अब सौ मतलब निकलेंगे आपके जाने के बाद...

vichalit

khabar thee gareebo.n kee bastee me.n khushiyaa.n Chhaa-ee.n hai.n
imaarato.n me.n kuChh be-chai-nee see f-ai-l gayee

Unsettling

News arrived;
"A sheen of happiness covers the slums."
A mild unease spread itself amongst the men of means.

vichalit = विचलित = disturbed
bechainee = बेचैनी = unease

विचलित

खबर थी ग़रीबों की बस्ती में खुशियाँ छाई हैं
इमारतों में कुछ बेचैनी सी फैल गयी...

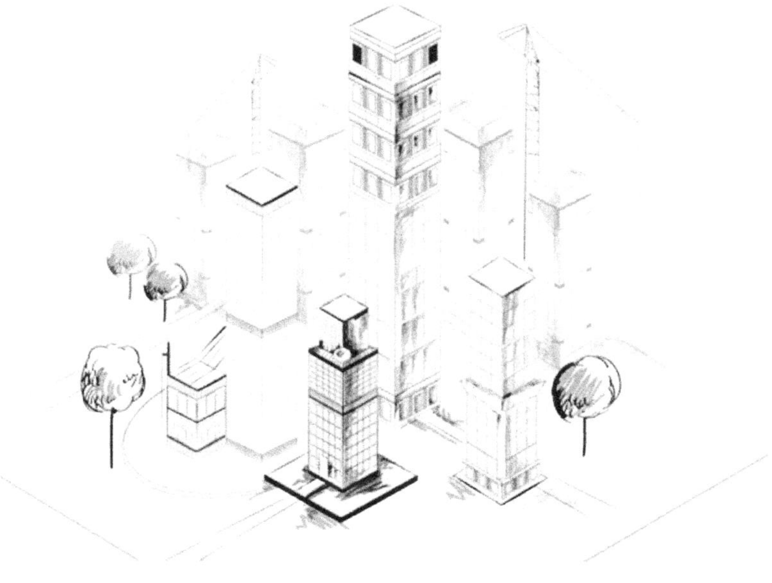

gumraah

un ChhoTe logo.n se mat pooChh zindagee kaa naam
wo... jo gum hai.n apnee hee benaamee ke gam me.n...

Pusillanimous

Do not query these small-minded men about the largesse of Life...
They... who are weighed down in grief...
by their mere anonymity in this world...

gumraah = गुमराह = one who has lost his way; misguided

गुमराह

उन छोटे लोगों से मत पूछ ज़िंदगी का नाम
वो... जो गुम हैं अपनी ही बेनामी के ग़म में...

aa b-ai-l…

do gehoo.n ke daane chal rahe the
insaano.n kee soch liye
ek sone ke sil-baTTe kee talaash me.n

Blinkers

With a very human lot of desires they started,
these two grains of wheat...
in a serious quest to be grist
for a pair of golden millstones…

sil-baTTaa = सिल–बट्टा = grindstones

आ बैल

दो गेहूँ के दाने चल रहे थे
इंसानों की सोच लिए
एक सोने के सिल–बट्टे की तलाश में...

udhaar

ek chavannee kho ga-ee meree jeb se
ab saahookaar bhookhaa reh jaa-e-gaa

Misplaced Hunger

A penny was lost from my pocket today.
Alas! the usurer will suffer now the pangs of hunger…

udhaar = उधार = a loan
chavannee = चवन्नी = a coin of value 25 paise = 0.25 Indian rupee
saahookaar = साहूकार = userer; money-lender

उधार

एक चवन्नी खो गयी मेरी जेब से
अब साहूकार भूखा रह जाएगा...

bikhre se...

ye chaand har roz TukDo.n TukDo.n me.n jeetaa hai
shaayad wo bhee kabhee kisee kee aarzoo rahaa thaa...

Phased Out

This phasing moon, it lives out its days in shattered bits and pieces;
perhaps it, too, was once someone's (now sundered) Desire...

bikhre = बिखरे = broken and scattered
aarzoo = आरज़ू = desire

बिखरे से...

ये चाँद हर रोज़ टुकड़ों टुकड़ों में जीता है
शायद वो भी कभी किसी की आरज़ू रहा था...

laalee

ye kisne sooraj me.n surkh aag lagaa dee hai
zamee.n par behtaa lahoo doobte aasmaa.n me.n rees gayaa hai...
ab too hee bataa kyaa rang laa-e-gee ye Dhaltee saanjh…

Ichor

Who has ignited the evening sun in a vermillion fire?
The sanguinary rivulets of earthly blood-shed
have seeped into the melting sky…
Pray, tell me, what omens this sinking evening portends…

surkh = सुर्ख़ = fiery red
rees gayaa = रीस गया = mingled deeply
saanjh = साँझ = evening

लाली

ये किसने सूरज में सुर्ख आग लगा दी है
ज़मीं पर बहता लहू डूबते आसमाँ में रीस गया है...
अब तू ही बता क्या रंग लाएगी ये ढलती साँझ...

behtaa sookhaa

kal akasmaat hee do rote aa.nsoo.n ghir aaye aa.nkho.n me.n
bahaane kaa bahaanaa Dhoo.nDhte
hamne bhee beetee jawaanee yaad kar lee chupke se

A Flowing Famine

A couple of tear drops ambushed my eyes yesterday.
For an excuse to shed them,
I quietly recalled the memories of youth past...

sookhaa = सूखा = famine
akasmaat = अकस्मात = without warning; suddenly = अचानक

बहता सूखा

कल अकस्मात ही दो रोते आँसू घिर आए आँखों में
बहाने का बहाना ढूँढते
हमने भी बीती जवानी याद कर ली चुपके से

aarzoo-e-manzil

yoo.n to aasmaan se sitaaro.n ko toD laane kee baat thee
tamannaa-o.n kee sarhado.n se paar jaane kee baat thee,
ye baat kuChh aur rahee
ke zindagee ke naap-taul ne roke rak-khaa;
varnaa un sitaaro.n ke peeChhe Chhupe
armaano.n ko paane kee baat thee…

Leaded Flight

Oh, how lofty they were!… the soaring thoughts…
of reaching for the heavens,
and trespassing the boundaries
of mortal aspirations.

Alas! A different equation of thought unfolded,
as the daily measures of life exacted their toll,
and rolled out a prosaic fate...
…for what else could have stopped our embrace
of the ultramundane ambition
spanned by the faraway stars?

aarzoo = आरज़ू = desire
sarhad = सरहद = boundary; border
naap-taul = नाप–तौल = the act of weighing
tamannaa = तमन्ना = desire
armaan = अरमान = desire

आरज़ू-ए-मंज़िल

यूँ तो आसमान से सितारों को तोड़ लाने की बात थी
तमन्नाओं की सरहदों से पार जाने की बात थी,
ये बात कुछ और रही
के ज़िंदगी के नाप–तौल ने रोके रक्खा;
वरना उन सितारों के पीछे छुपे
अरमानों को पाने की बात थी...

honee-anhonee

har do raahe par shuru hotee hai
ek kahaa.nee
ek ankahee

Said-Unsaid

At every fork in the road,
a story unfolds...
beside a story untold…

honee = होनी = that which happens
anhonee = अनहोनी = that which does not, or cannot, happen
doraahaa = दोराहा = fork in the road

होनी - अनहोनी

हर दोराहे पर शुरू होती है
एक कहानी
एक अनकही...

gatirodh

mat ruk soch kar ye zindagee tham see gayee hai
kuChh jharne ban jaate hai.n aabshaar chalte chalte

With The Flow...

Think not your life has stagnated at its gentle pace.
Many a brook gathers up a cataract on its way.

gatirodh = गतिरोध = that which obstructs speed; speed-breaker
jharnaa = झरना = a stream; a brook
aabshaar = आबशार = an enormous waterfall; also called "jalprapaat" = जलप्रपात in Hindi

गतिरोध

मत रुक सोच कर ये ज़िंदगी थम सी गयी है
कुछ झरने बन जाते हैं आबशार चलते चलते...

paraa-ee aas

mat pee kisee aur kee pyaas
maa.n kehtee thee tab
mai.n to samajh n sakaa
us mrigjal kee aaD me.n
shaayad tum hee yaad rakhlo
meree is bhool ko...

Borrowed Desire

"Do not drink someone else's thirst!",
mother would admonish me cryptically.

Alas! Never did I understand that wisdom...

Blinded by the reflections of these mirages,
I failed to grasp its essence....

Perhaps my error may serve to be your reminder.

mrigjal = मृगजल = mirage
aaD = आड़ = behind an object. "veil", in this context

पराई आस

मत पी किसी और की प्यास
माँ कहती थी तब
मैं तो समझ न सका
उस मृगजल की आड़ में
शायद तुम ही याद रख लो
मेरी इस भूल को...

ummeed

aisaa ho aaj fir us khat kaa jawaab n aaye
bekaraaree kee dehleez par
ummeed barkaraar reh jaa-e...

Delicate Balance

One wishes, once again,
the fervent missive invites no response today,
and leaves undying hope in balance,
on the door-steps of eager impatience…

dehleez = दहलीज़ = door-sil; entrance floor of a door

उम्मीद

ऐसा हो
आज फिर उस खत का जवाब न आए
बेकरारी की दहलीज़ पर
उम्मीद बरकरार रह जाए...

vo sawaal

har manzil ek hee sawaal kartee hai
jo sochaa thaa toone
kyaa wahee hoo.n mai.n?

Interrogative

Every destination,
every goal-post,
every milestone
at the end of a desired fruition
asks but one question:

"Am I all that you had hoped I would be?"

वो सवाल

हर मंज़िल एक ही सवाल करती है
जो सोचा था तूने
क्या वही हूँ मैं?

pighaltaa ehsaas

wo yaad
jo ek guzre lamhe kee tarah jamee hu-ee thee kisee kone me.n
halkee see aa.nch me.n pighal kar aa.nkho.n tak aa gayee
khushee kaa pal thaa
ek biChhaDe yaar se mile the jaise
jaane kyo.n
duniyaa ko lagaa ham ro rahe.n hai.n

Teared Memory

That distant memory,
a frozen moment in a mental recess,
melted at the light heat of remembrance,
and flowed its way into the eyes.

t'was a moment of simple joy,
a reunion of lost companions.
I wonder why the world engages a narrow vision,
and sees it as grieved weeping...

pighaltaa = पिघलता = melting
ehsaas = एहसास = feeling of awareness
aa.nch = आँच = heat of a flame

पिघलता एहसास

वो याद
जो एक गुज़रे लम्हे की तरह जमी हुई थी किसी कोने में
हल्की सी आँच में पिघल कर आँखों तक आ गयी
खुशी का पल था
एक बिछड़े यार से मिले थे जैसे
जाने क्यों
दुनिया को लगा हम रो रहें हैं

feeke pakwaan

oo.nchee imaarat
ChhoTaa darwaazaa
isme.n aadmee rehtaa hai
yaa bau-naa?

Facade

Such small doors
in such tall houses!
Do men live here
or pygmies?

feeke = फीके = bland; with no sweetness
pakwaan = पकवान = sweets
bau-naa = बौना = a dwarf

फीके पकवान

ऊँची इमारत
छोटा दरवाज़ा
इसमें आदमी रहता है
या बौना?

badlaa zamaanaa

pehle dauD-tee thee uma.ngo.n kee hawaa-e.n mere muhal-le me.n
ab logo.n ne darwaazaa band rakhnaa seekh liyaa hai

Evolving Times

In vintage days past,
the merry breeze of brotherhood swirled -
vibrant and unrestrained -
in our village...
Now, in these changing times,
people have learned to hide behind closed doors.

uma.ng = उमंग = exhilarating desire
zamaanaa = ज़माना = the world

बदला ज़माना

पहले दौड़ती थी उमंगों की हवाएँ मेरे मुहल्ले में
अब लोगों ने दरवाज़ा बंद रखना सीख लिया है...

akhiyo.n ke jharokho.n se

kitnaa karogee baate.n inse
ab to aa.nkhe.n band kar lo
khaamosh rehne do un nigaaho.n ko
kahee.n kahaanee naa ban jaa-e vaise hee

The Silence Of Those Eyes!

Your alluring eyes,
Oh! how they speak! How they speak!!
Shield the world from their assault, Love;
rein in their galloping thoughts;
but for their silence,
a living saga might unfold,
here and now…

jharokhaa = झरोखा = a small window; a peep-hole
nigaah = निगाह = eye
khaamosh = खामोश = silence; silent

अँखियों के झरोखों से

कितना करोगी बातें इनसे
अब तो आँखें बंद कर लो
खामोश रहने दो उन निगाहों को
कहीं कहानी ना बन जाए वैसे ही

baharhaal...

koi itihaas ke panno.n se pooChhe
jo huaa
kyaa wo sab waajib thaa?

Querying History

Someone should query the pages of History:
Was all which happened... justified?

baharhaal = बहरहाल = in all cirumstances; sometimes used to say, "in any case"

itihaas = इतिहास = history

pannaa = पन्ना = a page

wajib = वाजिब = just; appropriate

बहरहाल...

कोई इतिहास के पन्नों से पूछे
जो हुआ
क्या वो सब वाजिब था?

ChhoTee see baat

kyo.n bikhar gayaa wo makaan
ek ee.nT hee to churaa-ee thee uskee nee.nv se...

Base Nature

Why did that house crumble and fall?
Did I steal more than a lowly brick from its foundation?

nee.nv = नींव = foundation
ee.nT = ईंट = brick

छोटी सी बात

क्यों बिखर गया वो मकान
एक ईंट ही तो चुराई थी उसकी नींव से...

kehnaa-sun-naa

lo
ye meree zubaa.n kaa karz kaano.n par rakh lo
aur band kar lo unhe.n
zamaanaa baDaa hee jhooThaa hai

Them Liars, All!

Here, let me lend you my earnest entreaties.
Accept them, and seal your ears forthwith;
let them hear no more of another's importuning love;
for this world....is replete with lies and liars...

zubaa.n = ज़ुबाँ = tongue

कहना-सुनना

लो
ये मेरी जुबाँ का कर्ज़ अपने कानों पर रख लो
और बंद कर लो उन्हें
ज़माना बड़ा ही झूठा है...

mukaablaa

toofaan aane ko hai
lagtaa hai
khudaa bachaa kar rahegaa aaj
samandar ko meree nav se

Contest

Watch! A storm brews over the ocean!
One wonders if the good Lord strives to shield the sea
from the spirit of my boat...

mukaablaa = मुकाबला = contest

मुकाबला

तूफान आने को है
लगता है
खुदा बचा कर रहेगा आज
समंदर को मेरी नाव से

(added by Mrs. Rajani Sharma (Chicago, USA):

"तूफान से कह दो सिमट जाए.
ऐसी नाव पे तो समंदर को नाज़ है"

"Command the storm to hold its winds.
For a boat of such pluck,
even the mighty sea bows in respect."

a-n-mi-le

nahee.n sambhaltaa ek khayaal kaa bojh
"kaash! vaisaa huaa hotaa…"

Unobtained

Oh! The pathos and longing in the blue heart,
as it laments,
"If only THAT had happened!…"

bojh = बोझ = weight; burden
kaash! = काश! = if only!

अनमिले

नहीं संभलता एक ख़याल का बोझ
"काश! वैसा हुआ होता..."

hataash

"kyaa diyaa mujhe is zindagee ne?"
karkash saa sawaal kiyaa
ek murdaa-dil khayaal ne

Half Empty

"Whatever has this worthless life given me?",
a lifeless thought queried querulously…

karkash = कर्कश = grating
murdaa = मुर्दा = dead; a corpse
murdaa-dil = मुर्दा–दिल = one without courage or will to live

हताश

"क्या दिया मुझे इस ज़िंदगी ने?"
कर्कश सा सवाल किया
एक मुर्दा–दिल ख़याल ने

la.ngar

ye kaunsee baat ChheDee usoolo.n kee, kambakht!
ab Thokar nahee.n maaree jaatee jaalee zamaane ko
ye bhaaree sikko.n kee moch hai
ab karaahte bhee ha.nste hu-e hai.n ham

Chains...

Why raise it,
this awkward question of principles?
(shouldn't you know better, you fool!?)

It is much too late
to abdicate this compromised world;
a sprain of lucre chains our ankles...
Perforce, amidst our groans,
are we forced to put up a smile…

la.ngar = लंगर = an anchor
Thokar = ठोकर = a kick
usool = उसूल = credo; personal principle of behavior
jaalee = जाली = counterfeit; fake
moch = मोच = sprain
karaahte = कराहते = groaning

लंगर

ये कौनसी बात छेडी उसूलों की, कम्बख़्त!
अब ठोकर नहीं मारी जाती जाली ज़माने को
ये भारी सिक्कों की मोच है
अब कराहते भी हँसते हुए हैं हम

eklaa chaalo re...

har shakhs ek kaarvaa.n khudee me.n
kisee aur ke jaane kaa gam kaisaa

The Lone Traveler

Each soul is a caravan in itself;
why grieve at someone else's departure?

eklaa = एकला = alone
chaalo = चालो = walk
shakhs = शख़्स = person
kaarvaa.n = कारवाँ = caravan

एकला चालो रे...

हर शख़्स एक कारवाँ खुदी में
किसी और के जाने का गम कैसा

eendhan

pooChho un dehekte angaaro.n se
kyaa jalaa-e.nge ye duniyaa jalaane ke baad

Burn-Out

Ask those smoldering embers
what they would wish to burn next,
once they've burned down this world…

eendhan = ईंधन = fuel
dehekte = दहकते = smoldering; burning

ईंधन

पूछो उन दहकते अंगारों से
क्या जलाएँगे ये
दुनिया जलाने के बाद...

kamsin khayaal

a.ngDaa-ee-yaa.n naa fe.nko us suljhe badan kee
be-chai.niyaa.n vaise hee uljhaa gayee hai.n khayaalo.n ko
sochtaa hoo.n ab kar loo.n dushmanee aap se
aur sulah me.n aa jaa-oo.n panaah me.n

Strategic Thought

Good Heavens!
Do not cat-stretch your sensuous body so!
As is, my thoughts, without provocation,
are a tangled heap...

Perhaps - so runs my intoxicated thought -
I should declare you the erstwhile enemy,
and seek your asylum in open surrender.

kamsin = कमसिन = sensual; not of age
suljhe = सुलझे = well-defined
badan = बदन = body
angdaa-ee = अंगड़ाई = cat-stretch; pandiculation
sulah = सुलह = truce
panaah = पनाह = asylum

कमसिन ख़याल

अंगड़ाईयाँ ना फेंको उस सुलझे बदन की
बेचैनियाँ वैसे ही उलझा गयी हैं ख़यालों को
सोचता हूँ अब कर लूँ दुश्मनी आप से
और सुलह में आ जाऊँ पनाह में...

u-soo-lo.n kee duniyaa

ar-e mat kar ummeed, jaahil!
ummeed pe duniyaa nahi.n, dhokaa kaayam hai

Preconditioned

Do not foster these desires, O uninitiated fool!
Hope Eternal does not sail these waters...
only the lever of infernal deceit
turns on this fulcrum of expectations.

usool = उसूल = credo; personal principle of behavior
jaahil = जाहिल = uneducated; uninitiated fool = अज्ञानी, मूर्ख, बेवक़ूफ़

उसूलों की दुनिया

अरे मत कर उम्मीद, जाहिल!
उम्मीद पे दुनिया नहीं, धोका कायम है...

mailee miT-Tee

in kheto.n se kin faslo.n kee aas rakhoo.n
is miTTee ko dekh ab too hee bataa...

Soiled

What manner of harvest should I expect from this land?
Inspect this soil with care, my friend,
and then render your judgment...

mailee = मैली = coated with dirt; adulterated
miTTee = मिट्टी = soil
fasal = फसल = crop

मैली मिट्टी

इन खेतों से किन फसलों की आस रखूँ
इस मिट्टी को देख अब तू ही बता...

bojh

koi in kaandho.n par rakhaa patthar
dil par dhar de
jagah banaa de thoDee un par
kal janaazaa uThaanaa hai apnee aarzuo.n kaa

Hearse Rehearsal

Someone please shift this burden
from my shoulders down to my heart...
to this hearse I need lend my shoulders;
'tis a funeral to burn out my soul's desires.

dhar de = धर दे = lay down forcefully
janaazaa = जनाज़ा = funeral procession; hearse; wake = अर्थी

बोझ

कोई इन कांधों पर रखा पत्थर
दिल पर धर दे
जगह बना दे थोड़ी उन पर
कल जनाज़ा उठाना है अपनी आरज़ुओं का...

jalne do

un jaltee chitaao.n ko to mat bujhaa-o
bin aag ke murdaa-dil vaise bhee ka-ee hai.n is sheher me.n

Bonfire

Do not douse those flaming pyres!

Where else would that fire reside
in this land full of dead-hearted souls
with cold bellies?

chitaa = चिता = pyre
murdaa-dil = मुर्दा–दिल = one without courage or will to live

जलने दो

उन जलती चिताओं को तो मत बुझाओ
बिन आग के मुर्दा–दिल वैसे भी कई हैं इस शहर में...

lahoo soyaa saa

ye aakrosh itnaa sust kyo.n hai?
kyo.n baiThaa hai man me.n jugaalee kartaa?
be-hi.nsaa, bezaar
bharee dopahar me.n booDhe bhai.nse saa
kyo.n rukaa hai
kee kisee aur kaa aakrosh
moo.nh kholegaa aawaaz lagaane?

Sleeping Dog

Why is this agony,
this torment,
this despair,
so indolent in its expression?
Without fiery lashings,
enervated,
supine as an old buffalo chewing cud
in the dead of the afternoon...

For what does it wait, this internal rebellion?

Has it wagered its supine hope
on someone else's distress
to rebel and redress the persecutions of life?

aakrosh = आक्रोश = angry internal rebellion; lashing out of angry sentiment
jugaalee = जुगाली = act of chewing cud
behi.nsaa = बेहिंसा = supine; without violence = बिना किसी हिंसक भाव से
bezaar = बेज़ार = unhappy; disinterested = मुँह फेरे हुए; नाखुश
bhai.nsaa = भैंसा = buffalo

लहू सोया सा

ये आक्रोश इतना सुस्त क्यों है?
क्यों बैठा है मन में जुगाली करता?
बेहिंसा, बेज़ार,
भरी दोपहर में बूढ़े भैंसे सा...
क्यों रुका है
की किसी और का आक्रोश
मुँह खोलेगा आवाज़ लगाने?

a.ngaare

kabhee is dil me.n tez aag dhadhaktee thee
ab uskee aa.nch thoDee neechee ho gayee hai
p-e-T me.n bastee hai ye ab
bin roTee ke eendhan par

Fire In The Belly

This heart, if you must know,
sported an intense furnace once;
in time's relentless grind,
the wick has lowered its tip;
it hides now in the sunken belly,
burning on the dry fuel of growling hunger...

dhadhaktee = धधकती = roiling; flaring intensely (typically in reference to fire)

aa.nch = आँच = heat of a flame

ee.ndhan = ईंधन = fuel

अँगारे

कभी इस दिल में तेज़ आग धधकती थी
अब उसकी आँच थोड़ी नीची हो गयी है
पेट में बसती है ये अब
बिन रोटी के ईंधन पर...

tiltil marte taare

kabhee dekhee hai tumne samandar par koi rukee hui leher?

mai.n-ne dekhee hai

mai.n dekhtaa hoo.n har roz
jab adnee see goliyaa.n
baapoo ke vichaaro.n ko Chhalnee kartee hai.n seene me.n

Riddled

Have you ever seen
a wave stationary on the ocean?

I have.

I see it every single moment around me,
as the trifling bullets of violence riddle
the heart of Mahatma's teachings…

leher = लहर = wave
Chhalnee = छलनी = sieve; riddled

तिलतिल मरते तारे

कभी देखी है तुमने समंदर पर कोई रुकी हुई लहर?

मैंने देखी है

मैं देखता हूँ हर रोज़
जब अदनी सी गोलियाँ
बापू के विचारों को छलनी करती हैं सीने में

rupahree

kis bakhoobee se chaandee kee chaadar oDhee hai duniyaa ne
door door tak dukhiyaaro.n ke aasaar hee nahee.n hai.n

Veneer

With such artful elegance does the world
drape itself in its silvery shawl...
as far as the vision stretches,
not a trace remains,
of shivering sorrow or poverty...

rupahree = रुपहरी = silvery
chaadar = चादर = sheet of cloth; a thin blanket
aasaar = आसार = signs of presence
dukhiyaaraa = दुखियारा = one suffering ongoing grief

रुपहरी

किस बखूबी से चाँदी की चादर ओढी है दुनिया ने
दूर दूर तक दुखियारों के आसार ही नहीं हैं...

sunvaaee

kal sunee thee hauslo.n kee fariyaad
aaj aasmaa.n kuChh simaT gayaa hai

Hearing

I gave a patient hearing to my aspirations yesterday;
today, the sky appears to have shrunk its expanse.

hauslaa = हौसला = confidence

simaTnaa = सिमटना = to lessen the span of embrace; to pull oneself in

सुनवाई

कल सुनी थी हौसलों की फरियाद
आज आसमाँ कुछ सिमट गया है...

laalsaa

ye samandar har roz
sone saa aaftaab nigal jaataa hai
fir bhee bechai.n rehtaa hai apnee had-o-hawas me.n
jaan paDtaa hai mantree hai koi hindustaan kaa

Avarice

This ocean... it swallows every eventide,
a bountiful ball of liquid gold;
yet, it squirms and churns ceaselessly,
restless in its endless greed;

Perhaps the ocean is a politician of India, as well....

aaftaab = आफ़ताब = sun
had = हद = boundary
hawas = हवस = greed
mantree = मंत्री = political leader

लालसा

ये समंदर हर रोज़
सोने सा आफ़ताब निगल जाता है
फिर भी बेचैन रहता है अपनी हद–ओ–हवस में
जान पड़ता है
मंत्री है कोई हिन्दुस्तान का

Chh-i-nn-Vi-Chh-i-nn

is nee.nd ke kooche-galiyo.n me.n bhee sone se dartaa hoo.n
sapno.n kaa sheeshaa har subah chubhte hu-e TooT-ta hai

Shattering

In the calm, winding corridors of slumber,
I fear the embrace of sleep,
for in every morning's wakefulness live
the myriad shards of shattered dreams.

Chh-i-nn-Vi-Chh-i-nn = छिन्न–विछिन्न = shattered and scattered
koochaa = कूचा = alleyway = गली
sheeshaa = शीशा = glass; mirror

छिन्न-विछिन्न

इस नींद के कूचे–गलियों में भी सोने से डरता हूँ
सपनों का शीशा हर सुबह चुभते हुए टूटता है

dhooriyaa.n

is duniyaa kee baarah dishaa-e.n
ek raam kee
das raavaN kee
aur ek wo
jo too chunegaa

Eightfold Way?

The worldly ways have twelve directions.
One is the righteous way of Lord Ram.
Ten are the facial windings of that demon, Ravan.
And one...
which you must chart for yourself...

dhooriyaa.n = धूरियाँ = axes; lines of a body's rotation

धूरियाँ

इस दुनिया की बारह दिशाएँ
एक राम की
दस रावण की
और एक वो
जो तू चुनेगा

pooChh-taaChh

naa uThaao hamaaree muhabbat kee shaan me.n koi sawaal
choT vaise hee gehree lagee hai unke jawaab se

Ask Not!

Interrogate not my burning passion, and besmirch its pride;
that love, which has suffered a mortal wound from her cold answer anyway.

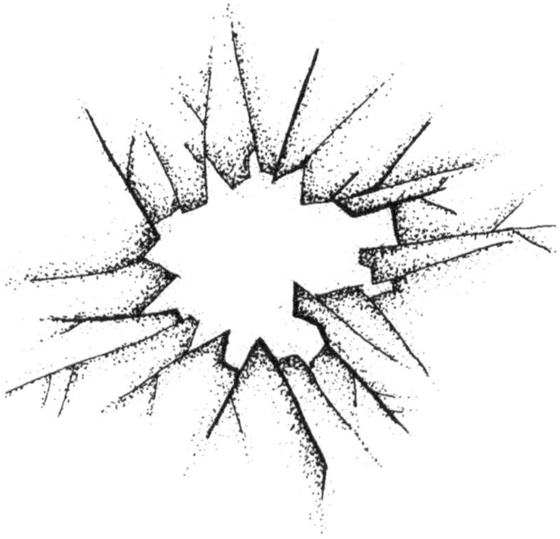

पूछ-ताछ

ना उठाओ हमारी मुहब्बत की शान में कोई सवाल
चोट वैसे ही गहरी लगी है उनके जवाब से

behtee shaam

beetee wo barsaat kee shaam
ek yaado.n kaa jharnaa beh gayaa

Evenstream

The evening was drenched in incessant rain.
A brook of memories was awash in its wake.

jharnaa = झरना = brook; a stream

बहती शाम

बीती वो बरसात की शाम
एक यादों का झरना बह गया

wo aate hee rahe

keh detee *"na"*, n aanaa thaa agar
ham to aadee the *"naa naa"* ke.
"dekhoo.ngee" keh diyaa na-haa.n me.n
yoo.n hee raah dekhte reh gaye umr bhar

Unrequited Hope

A simple *"no"* would have sufficed,
had you no intentions of visiting me...
I, who was comfortable in the collected string of *"no"*s...
"Maybe", you had replied casually.
Like a fool, I waited with bated breath all my life....

वो आते ही रहे

कह देती *"ना"*, न आना था अगर
हम तो आदी थे *"ना ना"* के
"देखूँगी" कह दिया ना–हाँ में
यूँ ही राह देखते रह गये उम्र भर...

aa-ee-ne ke sach

is shahar ke behte naalo.n me.n pratibimbit do sach
saDko.n kee sehmee gareebee kaa aks
aur aTTaalikaao.n ke naarehem kehkashe
ab is maile gehre paanee me.n naa Dhoo.nDh khudaa
iskee aagosh me.n khudaa-ee bhee kho gayee hai benaam

Reflected Truth

In the flowing gutters of this metropolis,
watch the reflections of two stalwart truths:
One, the rancid, emaciated poverty,
flailing and prostate by the roadside...
The other, a raucous, merciless laughter,
echoing in mockery across the sky-high hallways.

Why try to find Godhood
in these troubled waters?
In this overpowering, Augean filth,
even the angels have lost their divinity,
shuffling namelessly in Stygian depths...

pratibimbit = प्रतिबिंबित = reflected
aks = अक्स = image, reflection
aTTaalikaa = अट्टालिका = skyscraper
aagosh = आगोश = embrace
khudaa-ee = खुदाई = godhood
maile = मैले = muddied; dirty
benaam = बेनाम = anonymous; without a name

आईने के सच

इस शहर के बहते नालों में प्रतिबिंबित दो सच
सड़कों की सहमी ग़रीबी का अक्स
और अट्टालिकाओं के नारहम कहकशे
अब इस मैले गहरे पानी में ना ढूँढ खुदा
इसकी आगोश में खुदाई भी खो गयी है बेनाम

ek nazar

naa kar is husn kee tauheen, zaalim,
sirf ek nazar bhar dekh kar

Double Take

Dare not insult the ethereal beauty
of that heavenly body, you illiterate fool,
by quaffing its vision just this once!

husn = हुस्न = physical beauty
zaalim = ज़ालिम = one without mercy
tauheen = तौहीन = insult

एक नज़र

ना कर इस हुस्न की तौहीन, ज़ालिम,
सिर्फ़ एक नज़र भर देख कर

chand Tuk-De

jab TooT kar giraa aasmaa.n zamee.n par
sochaa nahee.n kiseene kayaamat aa-ee hai
chamkeele taare baTorne me.n mashgool
soch rahe the
shaayad khudaa bhee biktaa ho
...
yakeenan wo Theek sochte the

Thirty Pieces Of Silver

When the dome of the heavens cracked,
and fell resoundingly to the ground,
not one stopped to think
the Judgment Day had arrived.
Lost in gathering up the glittering stars, all,
they labored under the illusion
that even God could be corrupted and bought.
...
(now as I look back, I see)
there is no doubt they were right....

aasmaa.n = आसमाँ = dome of the sky
chand = चन्द = a few
mashgool = मशगूल = engrossed
baTorne me.n = बटोरने में = in the act of collecting
yakeenan = यक़ीनन = most certainly

चन्द टुकड़े

जब टूट कर गिरा आसमाँ ज़मीं पर
सोचा नहीं किसीने कयामत आई है
चमकीले तारे बटोरने में मशगूल
सोच रहे थे शायद खुदा भी बिकता हो
...
यक़ीनन वो ठीक सोचते थे

jeevan poo.njee

kyaa paayaa zindagee me.n
gar sanjoyaa sirf
ek silsilaa afsoso.n kaa…

Memorabilia

What have you accumulated in life,
if all you've strung together,
is a knotted string of regrets?

sanjoyaa = संजोया = collected and conserved
silsilaa = सिलसिला = sequence (usually, a sequence of events)

जीवन पूँजी

क्या पाया ज़िंदगी में
गर संजोया सिर्फ़
एक सिलसिला अफसोसों का...

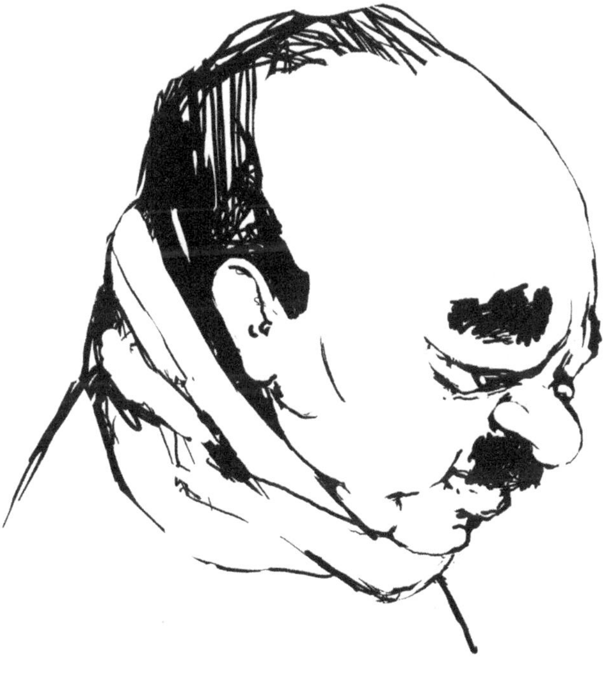

tinkaa-tinkaa

kuChh tinke sanjoye the mai.n-ne

kuChh mere dost le gaye apne gho.nsle banaane
kuChh beh gaye paanee me.n doobto.n ko bachaane me.n
aur kuChh jal gaye naakaam pyaar ke iraado.n me.n

ab kahaa.n se laa-u.n aur tinke gharaunde ke
saaree ghaas to jhulas gayee thee
piChhle saawan ke sooraj me.n

Burnt

It'was my wealth, those few straws I had conserved...

Some my friends borrowed to build their nests.
Some I used to save the drowning souls.
And some were burnt up in the fire of unrequited love.

Whither more straws for me to gather now?
All the dry grass I had counted on…
wasn't it all burnt up
in the heat of summer past?

tinkaa = तिनका = straw

gho.nslaa = घोंसला = nest

jhulasnaa = झुलसना = smolder and burn up

saawan = सावन = onset of monsoon season. In this context, the heat of monsoon season

तिनका-तिनका

कुछ तिनके संजोए थे मैंने

कुछ मेरे दोस्त ले गये अपने घोंसले बनाने
कुछ बह गये पानी में डूबतों को बचाने में
और कुछ जल गये नाकाम प्यार के इरादों में

अब कहाँ से लाऊं और तिनके घरौंदे के
सारी घास तो झुलस गयी थी
पिछले सावन के सूरज में

haal-e-ha.nsee

moo.nh n moDo is laaparwaahee se sun kar
baDee sanjeed-gee se paalaa hai hamne in lateefo.n ko

Humor Me

Please do not mock my humor with such facile contempt.
With all my seriousness have I nurtured this comical life.

moDo = मोडो = turn
laaparwahee = लापरवाही = carelessness
lateefaa = लतीफा = a joke
sanjeed-gee = संजीदगी = seriousness

हाले-हँसी

मुँह न मोडो इस लापरवाही से सुन कर
बड़ी संजीदगी से पाला है हमने इन लतीफों को

fir vahee

bastee jal gayee do pal me.n
saalo.n uTh-taa rahaa dhu-aa.n
aur lagaa gayaa na-ee aag
sau bastiyo.n me.n

Cyclic

In a few fiery moments,
the village burnt down to ashes,
but the embers,
they kept smoldering for years,
and in turn, they set afire
a hundred villages anew…

bastee = बस्ती = community (of people and houses)
dhu-aa.n = धुआँ = smoke

फिर वही

बस्ती जल गयी दो पल में
सालों उठता रहा धुआँ
और लगा गया नई आग
सौ बस्तियों में

ikraar-e-inkaar

tum mukar jaanaa agar koi pooChhe
kabhee tumhe mere pyaar se ikraar thaa
is raaz ko raaz hee rehne denaa
duniyaa jal jaa-e-gee jaan kar

Denial

Outright do deny, should they float a query,
if my love's ardor were ever requited;
keep your passion our own little secret.
The green fire of jealousy will smoke up your coveters...
were they to gather our furtive truth…

mukarnaa = मुकरना = to deny
ikraar = इकरार = acquiescence
inkaar = इनकार = refusal

इकरार-ए-इनकार

तुम मुकर जाना अगर कोई पूछे
कभी तुम्हे मेरे प्यार से इकरार था
इस राज़ को राज़ ही रहने देना
दुनिया जल जाएगी जान कर

doosraa sooraj

ab yahaa.n sooraj naa nikle to koi kamee nahee.n
wo dekho!
har jaltaa makaan
aaftaab saa saj rahaa hai sheher me.n

Burning Sun

No regrets
if the sun were not to rise on this land again.
There be no dearth of lumination now.
Look!
How every house in the city
burns as a miniature sun...

aaftaab = आफ़ताब = sun

दूसरा सूरज

अब यहाँ सूरज ना निकले तो कोई कमी नहीं
वो देखो!
हर जलता मकान
आफ़ताब सा सज रहा है शहर में

gehen masle

doodh-dahee to churaa le gaye lene waale
ye thoDaa gobar paDaa hai,
laDnaa ho to aa jao,
isee par behes kar le.nge

Point Of Contention

All the bounty of milk and cream,
now stolen property of thieves on the quick.
Here, we're left with the heaps of manure;
perhaps you wish to use them as the pretext
and continue our fierce arguments?

gobar = गोबर = cow-dung
behes = बहस = argument; debate

गहन मसले

दूध–दही तो चुरा ले गये लेने वाले
ये थोड़ा गोबर पड़ा है,
लड़ना हो तो आ जाओ,
इसी पर बहस कर लेंगे

mulzim-e-mehfil

mehfil me.n nazre.n churaa kar peenewaalaa
mere hisse kee ra.ngeenee Chheen kar pee rahaa ho jaise

Thief Of Drinks

In this vibrant, merry soiree, hark!
He who drinks with reservation so dry,
wastes my share of revelry on the sly.

mulzim = मुलज़िम = accused; criminal
mehfil = महफ़िल = gathering; a party, typically in the evening
ra.ngeenee = रंगीनी = colorfulness
Chheen kar = छीन कर = by snatching

मुलाज़िम-ए-महफ़िल

महफ़िल में नज़रें चुरा कर पीनेवाला
मेरे हिस्से की रंगीनी छीन कर पी रहा हो जैसे

junoon

apnee shahaadat ko ek naam de jaa jaahil
sirf muhabbat kahegaa to paagal jaane.nge log

A Rose By...

Anoint your martyrdom with a suitable moniker, you fool!
Call it just "Love",
and the world will brand you a lunatic...

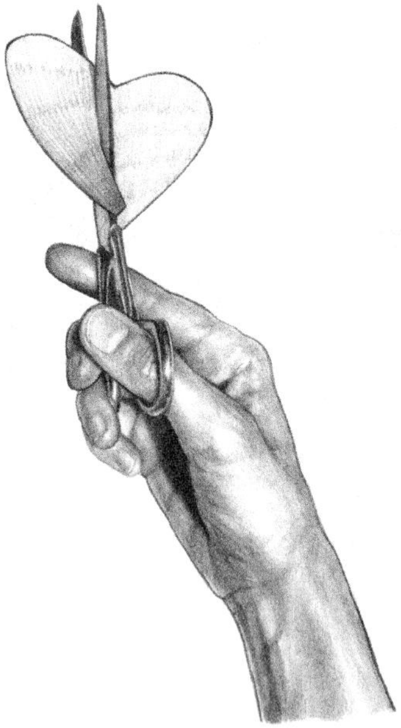

shahaadat = शहादत = martyrdom

junoon = जुनून = intense focus, mania, or mad intensity about something

जुनून

अपनी शहादत को एक नाम दे जा जाहिल
सिर्फ़ मुहब्बत कहेगा तो पागल जानेंगे लोग

roohaanee

ye rooh kis raah par reh gayee hai rehbar
rehmat nahee.n raahjanee hu-ee
rukhsat to hu-e the unse roo-ba-roo,
ab raah rok rahee hai rukhsaar kee yaad

Arrested

Where did I lose my soul on this path, O Companion?
Benign were those eyes engaged in this highway robbery...
Did I not depart her presence with all my senses, hale and hearty?
And here I am now, an arrested soul,
the visage of her memory
(and the memory of her visage)
shackling every step of mine...

rooh = रूह = soul, heart
rehbar = रहबर = confidant, guide, companion
rehmat = रहमत = mercy; largesse
raahjanee = राहज़नी = mugging; robbery
roobaroo = रूबरू = in person; face-to-face
rukhsaar = रुख़सार = visage; face

रूहानी

ये रूह किस राह पर रह गयी है रहबर
रहमत नहीं राहज़नी हुई
रुख़सत तो हुए थे उनसे रूबरू,
अब राह रोक रही है रुख़सार की याद

khaane dar khaane

ye to aapkee zarraa-nawaazee hai,
varnaa ham bhee ek hee khaane kee chaal ke pyaade hai.n

Elevation

Only the largesse of your heart elevates my humble being;
for truth be told, I be no more than a pawn
with a long reach spanning a mere square…

zarraa = ज़र्रा = an iota; a mote; inconsequential piece of matter

nawaazee = नवाज़ी = royal behavior

zarraa-nawaazee = ज़र्रा–नवाज़ी = elevation of an insignificant piece to royal status

khaanaa = खाना = a chessboard square (in this context)

pyaadaa = प्यादा = a pawn

खाने दर खाने

ये तो आपकी ज़र्रा–नवाज़ी है,
वरना हम भी एक ही खाने की चाल के प्यादे हैं

jeevan saritaa

kaun hawaa de rahaa hai umr-e-raftaa ko
zindagee ChhooTe jaa rahee hai
ab dauDoo.n aur tez
ya banaa-u.n jagah mukammal
tu hee bataa, ai yaad,
meree to fariyaad bhee
mujhse kahee.n aage nikal gayee hai

Flow Of Life

Who fans this breathless speed of my life?
This race, where Life slips relentlessly from my grasp?
Tell me, my friend:
should I run even faster to catch it?
Or should I make a place for repose right here?
Advise me, Memory mine!
For I feel helpless as I watch
even my plaintive desires outpace me in this strife...

umr-e-raftaa = उम्रे–रफ़्ता = speed of life
mukammal = मुकम्मल = fixed and safe
fariyaad = फरियाद = petition

जीवन सरिता

कौन हवा दे रहा है उम्रे–रफ़्ता को
ज़िंदगी छूटे जा रही है
अब दौड़ूँ और तेज़
या बनाऊँ जगह मुकम्मल
तू ही बता, ऐ याद,
मेरी तो फरियाद भी
मुझसे कहीं आगे निकल गयी है

chubhan

in kaaTo.n ko sameT kar rakh lo
ye sadaabahaar rehte hai.n
ik din kaam aa-e.n-ge
kisee tanahaa pal me.n

Prickly

Gather up these thorns carefully.
They never lose their freshness.
Someday, you will appreciate their kinship,
in a moment of lonesome melancholy…

sadaabahaar = सदाबहार = evergreen
kaa.nTe = काँटे = thorns
tanahaa = तनहा = lonesomeness
pal = पल = moment of time

चुभन

इन काँटों को समेट कर रख लो
ये सदाबहार रहते हैं
इक दिन काम आएँगे
किसी तनहा पल में

gam-Chhupaa

kyo.n apnee hatheleeyo.n pe ye khalish liye ghoomte ho
haath hilaane se wo gumshudaa hotee.n
to sabhee jaadoogar kehlaate...

Sleight Of Anguish

Why wear your prickly anguish on your sleeves, my friend?
If they could be waived away with the wave of a hand,
everyone here would be a sleight-of-hand magician...

khalish = खलिश = conundrum; uneasyness = परेशानी
gumshudaa = गुमशुदा = that which is lost

ग़म-छुपा

क्यों अपनी हथेलियों पे ये खलिश लिए घूमते हो
हाथ हिलाने से वो गुमशुदा होतीं
तो सभी जादूगर कहलाते...

ka-see-daa-kaa-ree

tum un TooTe sitaaro.n ko joD denaa
see denaa fir unhe raat kee chaadar me.n
rang denaa fir samaa.n apnee adaao.n se
kabhee khudaa bhee to dekhe tumhaaree kalaakaaree

Embroidery

Stitch together those broken stars;
Embroider them in the dark fabric of the night;
fling your palette of allure across the heavens;
let The Artist Herself behold your artistry…

ka-see-daa-kaa-ree = कसीदाकारी = embroidery
kalaakaaree = कलाकारी = artistry

कसीदाकारी

तुम उन टूटे सितारों को जोड़ देना
सी देना फिर उन्हे रात की चादर में
रंग देना फिर समाँ अपनी अदाओं से
कभी खुदा भी तो देखे तुम्हारी कलाकारी

nadaarad

wo baat ghoomtee rahee zehen me.n
aur zehen me.n hee kahee.n kho gayee
ab Dhoo.nDhtaa hoo.n roz use
miltee nahee.n
par pataa hai wo hai yahee.n kahee.n
intazaar me.n mere

Mislaid

That mental admonishment
kept reverberating in my conscience,
and somewhere in its labyrinth,
lost its wayward way, unnoticed...

To no avail, my desire to rediscover it;
it eludes me, that one single thought...
I sense its presence, though,
somewhere right beside me,
as if waiting
for me to find myself...

zehen = ज़हन = inner mind

नदारद

वो बात घूमती रही ज़हन में
और ज़हन में ही कहीं खो गयी
अब ढूँढता हूँ रोज़ उसे
मिलती नहीं
पर पता है वो है यहीं कहीं
इंतज़ार में मेरे

chai-n-bansee

us masjid ke ird-gird ghoomtaa rahaa allaah
jab ka-ee sau Dher ho rahe the maidaan-e-mulk me.n

Nero-In-The-Sky

Allah maintained His sacred presence around that mosque.
Of little consequence, alas,
that hundreds were being felled in his world,
in the cold blood of communal feud…

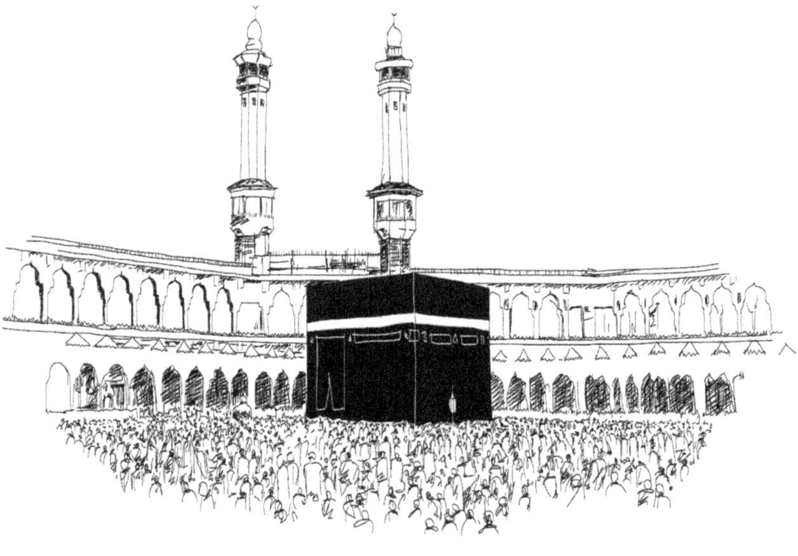

chain-bansee = चैन–बंसी = a flute on which you play the tunes of contentment and leisure

Dher honaa = ढेर होना = to die in combat; to be felled

maidaan-e-mulk = मैदान–ए–मुल्क = the open fields or playground of a country

चैन-बंसी

उस मस्जिद के इर्द–गिर्द घूमता रहा अल्लाह
जब कई सौ ढेर हो रहे थे मैदान–ए–मुल्क में

farmaanee pyaade

saaree kaa-i-naat kaa dard
apne befikr zehen me.n sameTe
khudaa gaur farmaa rahaa hai
apne agle mohre kee chaal

Insignificant Pawns

Coddling in His carefree heart
the hurt and sorrow of all His Creation,
the good Lord is, with infinite care,
reviewing another strategic move for his pawn.

farmaanee = फरमानी = varrying a decree or pronouncement
kaa-i-naat = काइनात = Creation
mohra = मोहरा = a chess piece
gaur farmaanaa = गौर फर्माना = mull; concentrate; evaluate

फरमानी प्यादे

सारी काइनात का दर्द
अपने बेफ़िक्र ज़हन में समेटे
खुदा गौर फ़र्मा रहा है
अपने अगले मोहरे की चाल

ab rehne de

ye dil unpe aayaa thaa kabhee
kab, kahaa.n, kaise
mat kar tauheen us yaad kee pooChh kar

Leave It Be

Yes, she did arrest my heart once..
When? Where? How?
Malign not that memory with philistine inquiries.

tauheen = तौहीन = insult

अब रहने दे

ये दिल उनपे आया था कभी
कब, कहाँ, कैसे
मत कर तौहीन उस याद की पूछ कर

likhaaee

likhne waale takdeer khud likh gaye
bakee paDhe-likhe paDh bhee naa sake
takdeer ke ishaaro.n ko...

Literacy

The true writers of life…they wrote their own destinies,
and moved on without a fuss;
those educated others...
they read not even the clues Fate wrote...
...between her decreed lines…

takdeer = तक्दीर = fate

लिखाई

लिखने वाले तक़दीर खुद लिख गये
बाकी पढ़े–लिखे पढ़ भी ना सके
तक़दीर के इशारों को...

bin piye

zindagee kaa lutf hai abhee baakee
shaam baakee, ulfat baakee,
nazre.n baakee, nazro.n kee sharaarat bhee baakee

itnee pee hai hamne
ke khumaar unpe chaDh jaa-e
par dekh yahaa.n saakee
abhee pyaale me.n jaam hai baakee

Intoxication Vicarious

Such choices of pleasures remain unsavored!
The amorous evening grows young;
infatuation spreads its drunken mist,
and coquettish eyes conspire...

Stoked with this wine I am, all drunk,
but it is she who looks intoxicated;
and such surprise, my dear sommelier!
this goblet of mine remains as yet untouched!

lutf = लुत्फ़ = pleasure
ulfat = उल्फ़त = love
khumaar = खुमार = intoxication
saakee = साकी = sommelier; keeper and server of wines

बिन पिए

जि़ंदगी का लुत्फ़ है अभी बाकी
शाम बाकी,
उल्फ़त बाकी,
नज़रें बाकी,
नज़रों की शरारत भी बाकी

इतनी पी है हमने
के खुमार उनपे चढ़ जाए
पर देख यहाँ साकी
अभी प्याले में जाम है बाकी...

hit-chin-tak

jaane-anjaane jo giraa gayaa
wo to naadaan thaa
us se kyaa gilaa karoo.n?
unkee baat aur hai
jo mujhe girte dekh
ha.nste rahe

Well-Wishers

The one who tripped me by accident,
he was without malice;
what complaint can I have about him?
Not so with them…
they...
who mocked me with laughter as I fell...

hit-chin-tak = हितचिंतक = well-wisher
naadaan = नादान = ingenuous; not wise of worldly ways
gilaa = गिला = complaint

हितचिंतक

जाने–अनजाने जो गिरा गया
वो तो नादान था
उस से क्या गिला करूँ?
उनकी बात और है
जो मुझे गिरते देख
हँसते रहे...

jo reh gayaa…

doobta sooraj doob gayaa
kal aane kaa vaada kar ke
ChhoD gayaa ye andheraa
aur chand maayoos taare...
kuChh unkee tarah…

Remainder...

The setting sun set in its due course,
with long promises of return,
leaving behind this darkness,
with its scattered, morose stars...
so reminiscent
of my separation from her…

maayoos = मायूस = sad

जो रह गया...

डूबता सूरज डूब गया
कल आने का वादा कर के
छोड़ गया ये अंधेरा
और चंद मायूस तारे...
कुछ उनकी तरह...

haale bedilee

kuChh pooChhe.n to bole
naa pooChh haal-e-jigar
jo chup hu-e to kehte hai.n
aisee bhee kyaa b-e-dilee

Ask Not

Solicit his affairs of heart,
and his despondency protests: *"Don't ask!"*
Absent the inquiry, he wails,
"Why be so heartless, my friend?"!

bedilee = बेदिली = disinterest

haale bedilee = हाले–बेदिली = disinterested in the state of someone's heart or mind

haal-e-jigar = हाले–जिगर = state of the heart

हाले-बेदिली

कुछ पूछें तो बोले
ना पूछ हाले–जिगर
जो चुप हुए तो कहते हैं
ऐसी भी क्या बेदिली

aafat

raaste par chaltaa ek gaD-Dhaa gir paDaa
aur choT lagee zameen ko…

Negative Energy

It was the do-nothing pothole which tripped and fell.
It was the guiding road which got hurt…

aafat = आफ़त = calamity; misfortune

आफ़त

रास्ते पर चलता एक गड्ढा गिर पड़ा
और चोट लगी ज़मीन को...

aa.nkh mi-chau-lee

koi kuChh kehtaa nahee.n bematlab
bas unke sivaa...
wo...
jo matlab Chhupaane ke maahir hai.n

Veiled Interest

No one speaks without an interest of self at heart.
Except her...
She... who is skilful
at veiling the interests of her heart.

matlab = मतलब = The word has 2 separate meanings:

1. essence; understanding; meaning
2. self-interest; selfishness

maahir = माहिर = expert

आँख-मिचौली

कोई कुछ कहता नहीं बेमतलब
बस उनके सिवा..
वो...
जो मतलब छुपाने के माहिर हैं

ek baat ai-see bhee

ye ha.nsee kabhee haaree nahee.n meree umr se
ke is dil me.n
har ghaDee
har saa.ns
har dam
ek jaa.n-mard ne hee apnaa pataa rakkha hai

Evergreen

My smile never surrendered to my age,
for in this heart,
in every moment,
in every breath,
in every beat,
none but a brave-heart
has ever declared its residence.

jaa.n-mard = जाँ–मर्द = a brave man with a daring heart

एक बात ऐसी भी

ये हँसी कभी हारी नहीं मेरी उम्र से
के इस दिल में
हर घड़ी
हर साँस
हर दम
एक जाँ-मर्द ने ही अपना पता रक्खा है

bheegee palke.n

zaalim jo ek nazar bhar naa dee parwaane ko
jab jal rahee thee shamaa bekaraaree kee
jo khaak ho gaye unkee mohabbat me.n
ab aa.nsoo bahaate hai.n hamaaree raakh par

Immolated

Tormentor mine, observe the irony...
you, who never spared a sliding glance for my covetous sighs
when the wildfire of desire was blazing high...
Now, when your conflagration has seared my soul in its flash,
you shed your tears on dying embers, and acrid, lust-less ash.

parwaanaa = परवाना = moth
shamaa = शमा = flame
bekaraaree = बेकरारी = without solace; impatience
khaak = ख़ाक = burnt down
raakh = राख = ash

भीगी पलकें

ज़ालिम जो एक नज़र भर ना दी परवाने को
जब जल रही थी शमा बेकरारी की
जो ख़ाक हो गये उनकी मोहब्बत में
अब आँसू बहाते हैं हमारी राख पर

Appendix - A Primer On Hindi

Devnagari Script & Transliteration

Reading Hindi Script & *Hindi-In-English*

Devnagari - The Script

Devnagari - literally meaning *"belonging to the city of the Gods"* - is the name of the alphabet and script behind dozens of Indian languages, including Hindi and Marathi. It has 42 commonly used letters (and 3-5 other letters which are now nearly defunct). There are some variations in the alphabet to accommodate nuances of various languages.

The letters in the alphabet are characterized by a header line from which the letters hang down. Each letter has a sound associated with it.

The sound of a given letter can be modified by a few types of modifiers (called *"maatraa"*):

- a vertical line, a dot or a semi-colon following the letter;
- placement of one or two slanted lines, a dot, a semi-circle, a dotted semi-circle, a turned semi-circle or a slanted line with a side dot above the header line;
- a slanted line below a letter to clip its sound;
- a dot below a letter to add a slight lisp or softening sound;
- a caret sign below a letter to add the "r" sound (to some letters).

In many cases, where sounds of 2 separate letters are to be merged, the first letter is cropped and merged with the second letter in writing. e.g. "tva" ("त्व") is a combination of "t" ("त") and "va" ("व").

A combination of letters and modifiers produces a very rich set of sounds.

It should be noted that the Devnagari script does not use a full stop to demarcate the end of a sentence but a vertical line, like "।"

Finally, a word on *Shayari*. *Shayari* is a form of verses which predominantly uses the Urdu language. The Urdu script is substantially different from Devnagari (and goes from right to left). However, phonetically, Urdu and Hindi share much commonality, in addition to a reasonable amount of vocabulary. In this book, all Urdu words have been represented in Devnagari, as is accepted practice.

Devnagari Alphabet

English	Devnagari Base Letter	Pronunciation
a	अ	Starting sound in "against"
i	इ	Clipped "ee" sound, as in "lit"
ee	ई	Starting sound in "keep"
u	उ	A clipped "oo" sound
oo	ऊ	The Starting sound in "ooze"
ru	ऋ	Starting sound in "ruminate"
ae	ए	Starting sound in "aim"
ai	ऐ	Starting sound in "air"
k	क	Starting sound in "cut"
kh	ख	Starting sound in "Khalifa", as in "Burj Khalifa"
g	ग	Starting sound in "go"
gh	घ	Combination of 2 sounds: "g" and "h"
ch	च	Starting sound in "chatter"
Chh	छ	Combination of 2 sounds: "ch" and "h"
j	ज	Starting sound in "jug"
jh, z	झ	Last sound in "maze"
T	ट	Starting sound in "try"
Th	ठ	Combination of 2 sounds: "T" and "h"
D	ड	Starting sound in "dog"
Dh	ढ	Combination of 2 sounds: "D" and "h"
t	त	The starting sound in "Talmud" or the French "tu"
th	थ	Starting sound in "three" or "thunder"
d	द	Same as the British pronunciation of English word, "the"
dh	ध	Combination of 2 sounds: "d" and "h"
n	न	Starting sound in "no"
p	प	Starting sound in "punch"
f	फ	Starting sound in "first"
b	ब	Starting sound in "burn"

bh	भ	Combination of 2 sounds: "b" and "h"
m	म	Starting sound in "mother"
y	य	Starting sound in "yearn"
r	र	Starting sound in "run"
l	ल	Starting sound in "loud"
v	व	Starting sound in "viral"
sh	श	Starting sound in "shut"
Sh	ष	Starting sound in "shut"
s	स	Starting sound in "sound"
h	ह	Starting sound in "hunger"
N	ण	This has no English equivalent or combination. It is a strong "n". Make the "n" sound with the tip of the tongue touching the palate (the roof of the mouth) That is "N"
dnya	ज्ञ	Combination of 2 sounds: "g" and "y". In some languages like Marathi, it is a combination 3 sounds: "d", "n" and "ya"
tra	त्र	Combination of 3 sounds: "t", "r" and "a"

Modifications of base letters by "maatraa": showing an example using " र "

Combination	**Modified**	**Devnagari Letter**
r	र	
ra	रा	
ri	रि	
ree	री	
ru	ऋ	Can also be used as "kru"
roo	रू	
re	र	
rai	र	
ro	रो	
rau	रौ	Combination of 2 sounds: "r" and "au"
raw	रॉ	
rr	र्र	
ram	रं	Pronounced "rum"
ram	रँ	Pronounced "rum"
r-haa	रः	
ku	कु	Showing lower maatraa with "क" as they don't appear in this bottom location for "र"
koo	कू	

Made in the USA
Monee, IL
05 November 2026

67951436R00105